M000043939

TO:_____

FROM:_____

Published by Sellers Publishing, Inc.

161 John Roberts Road, South Portland, ME 04106

Visit us at www.sellerspublishing.com • E-mail: rsp@rsvp.com

© 2016 Sellers Publishing, Inc.

Artwork & Design © 2016 Primitives by Kathy®

ISBN-13: 978-1-4162-4601-5

Printed and bound in China.

10 9 8 7 6 5 4 3 2 1

A DOG WAGS ITS TAIL WITH ITS HEART

A DOG WAGS ITS TAIL WITH ITS HEART

LIFE WITHOUT DOGS...
I DON'T THINK SO

LIFE IS JUST BETTER WHEN I'M WITH MY DOG

A DOG DOESN'T CARE IF YOU ARE RICH OR POOR GIVE A DOG YOUR HEART AND HE'LL GIVE YOU HIS

SORRY I CAN'T

I HAVE PLANS

WITH MY DOG

I WORK HARD SO MY DOG CAN HAVE A BETTER LIFE

THERE IS NO TROUBLE
SO GREAT THAT
CANNOT BE
DIMINISHED BY
DOG KISSES

LORD PLEASE HELP ME
BE THE PERSON
MY DOG
THINKS I AM

ALL YOU NEED IS LOVE... AND A DOG

DOGS LEAVE PAW PRINTS ON YOUR HEART FOREVER

LIFE IS SHORT
PLAY WITH
YOUR DOG

I WISH THE DOG HAD A SNOOZE BUTTON

I DON'T NEED THERAPY ... I HAVE A DOG

YOU CAN GET TRUE LOVE FROM SOME HUMANS AND ALL DOGS

ALWAYS KISS YOUR DOG GOODNIGHT

PLEASE REMOVE YOUR SHOES THE DOG NEEDS SOMETHING TO CHEW ON

I BELIEVE IN SANTA PAWS

I JUST WANT TO DRINK WINE & PET MY DOG

I SLEEP WITH DOGS

IN DOG BEERS

BEERS

I'VE ONLY HAD ONE

KISS YOUR DOG DAILY

WAG MORE
BARK LESS

LOVE ME
LOVE MY DOG

MY DOG WALKS ALL OVER ME

ONE DOG AWAY FROM BEING A DERANGED DOG LADY

RING DOOR BELL WIN A DOG

SAVING ONE DOG WILL
NOT CHANGE THE WORLD
BUT SURELY FOR THAT
ONE DOG, THE WORLD
WILL CHANGE FOREVER

THIS HOUSE IS MAINTAINED ENTIRELY FOR THE COMFORT AND CONVENIENCE OF THE DOG

WHEN I DIE THE DOG GETS EVERYTHING